Examining Canadian Energy

Examining

Water Power

Anne Garcia

SAUNDERS
BOOK COMPANY

Published by Saunders Book Company
27 Stewart Road, Collingwood, ON Canada L9Y 4M7

www.saundersbook.ca

Produced by Red Line Editorial

Library and Archives Canada Cataloguing in Publication

Garcia, Anne, author
        Examining water power / Anne Garcia.

(Examining Canadian energy)
Includes bibliographical references and index.
Issued in print and electronic formats.
ISBN 978-1-77092-276-1 (bound).--ISBN 978-1-77092-284-6 (pbk.).--
ISBN 978-1-77092-292-1 (html)

        1. Water-power--Canada--Juvenile literature. I. Title. II. Title:
Water power. III. Series: Examining Canadian energy

TC146.G37 2014   j333.9'140971   C2014-903561-6
                                               C2014-903562-4

Picture Credits

Capture Light/Shutterstock Images, cover, 1; Martin Lehmann/Shutterstock
Images, 5; Pecold/Shutterstock Images, 8; Georgios Kollidas/Shutterstock Images,
9; jgorzynik/Shutterstock Images, 11; Jeremy Mayes/iStockphoto, 13; Ronnie
Chua/Shutterstock Images, 15; Jupiterimages/Thinkstock, 16; Terry Davis/
Shutterstock Images, 17; Dani Vincek/Shutterstock Images, 19; Todd Paris/
Alaska Power & Telephone Company/AP Images, 20; Red Line Editorial, 21; Peter
Wey/Shutterstock Images, 23; vvoe/Shutterstock Images, 25; Simplyphotos/
Thinkstock, 26–27; V. J. Matthew/Shutterstock Images, 28; EpicStockMedia/
Shutterstock Images, 31; HO/Finavera Renewables/AP Images, 32; Warren
Goldswain/Shutterstock Images, 34; Galyna Andrushko/Shutterstock Images, 36;
NOAA/Department of Commerce, 39; Lightpoet/Shutterstock Images, 41; Jaren
Jai Wicklund/Shutterstock Images, 45

Printed in the United States of America
Corporate Graphics Inc.
July 2014

Contents

CHAPTER 1

The Power of Water

Have you ever heard someone in your family complain about the high cost of electricity? People around the world use a lot of energy, and the demand for energy continues to rise. Right now, most of this energy comes from non-renewable sources, such as fossil fuels. Fossil fuels, such as oil, coal, and natural gas, can be bad for the environment. They also take millions of years to form, which means we are using them faster than they can be produced. Because of this, many scientists and innovators are trying to find ways to increase our use of alternative energy sources. Alternative energy sources include biofuels, wind energy, solar energy, and water power.

Water covers more than 70 percent of the earth's surface. About 96.5 percent of Earth's water comes from oceans. Only 2.5 percent of Earth's water is freshwater. It comes from

Moving water is a renewable resource we can use to generate energy without burning fossil fuels.

groundwater, glaciers, ice caps, lakes, and ice and snow melt. A tiny fraction is water vapour in the atmosphere.

We can harness the energy from moving water, such as rivers, ocean waves, and tides, to create energy we can use. Energy from moving water is clean and renewable. Water is not consumed during energy generation the way fossil fuels are when burned to create energy. Water can be used over and over again.

Converting water power to electricity does not pollute the environment. However, building hydroelectric facilities and manufacturing hydroelectric equipment, such as turbines and dams, does produce pollution. Still, the availability of water means it will play an important role in our future energy production.

EXPLORING WATER POWER

In this book, it is your job to learn about water power and its place in our future energy production. How did people use water power in the past? What kinds of moving water can we use to create energy? What kind of energy does water power give us? How do we use it now? How might we use water power in the future?

Zach Miller is part of a study group researching alternative energy for a science fair project. Zach's job is to learn about water power. He is conducting research and interviewing experts in the field to learn more about water power as an energy source. Reading Zach's journal will help you in your own research.

2,500 Years of Water Power

I decide to start my research by discussing how past cultures have used water power as an energy source. I stay after school to talk to my science teacher, Ms. Arnold. I'm surprised by how much she knows about the history of water power.

"Water power may be considered an alternative energy source today," Ms. Arnold says, "but humans have been harnessing the power of water for longer than you might think! Ancient records are fuzzy. But historians believe the ancient Chinese used water power to grind grain as early as the 100s BCE. Romans were the first to write about water-powered wheels, although it seems as if they didn't use them often—at least not until the 300s CE. Then they used 16 waterwheels to grind grain in what is now southern France. Waterwheels were an important source of energy throughout Europe from the 1000s on."

Humans have harnessed the energy of moving water for more than 1,000 years by using waterwheels such as this one in Czech Republic.

Ms. Arnold picks up a small pinwheel off her desk as she talks. "But it doesn't really matter who used water power first. What's important to know is that waterwheels operate much like this pinwheel I'm holding."

She blows on the pinwheel, and it spins.

"Air turns this pinwheel much like water turns a waterwheel. The mill uses the kinetic energy, or energy of motion, of the flowing water to turn the stones that grind the grain."

Ms. Arnold tells me that there are two basic types of waterwheels. They are called undershot and overshot. The undershot waterwheel is partially submerged in the river. Its grinding speed depends on the speed of the river as water flows by. A slow flow means slow grinding.

With overshot wheels, the water source comes from above. Gates above the wheel, known as sluice gates, control the flow of the water, which turns the wheel. The wheel drives a complicated set of gears that perform work, such as grinding wheat into flour, powering a sawmill, or pumping water.

"Thanks to Michael Faraday, a British chemist and physicist, hydropower, or power harnessed from water power, became a force for generating electricity in the late 1800s," Ms. Arnold tells me. She explains that his experiments led to the first generator to produce a steady electric current. His findings became the basis of hydroelectricity. In 1881, Ottawa Electric Light Co. built a small waterwheel on the Ottawa River. It was used to power lights. Within five years, hydroelectric power from Niagara Falls was being transmitted to Buffalo, New York. Throughout the early 1900s, many hydroelectric sites were built in Canada, mainly in Ontario and Quebec. Canada's first major hydroelectric facility was built at Shawinigan Falls, Quebec, in 1898. In 1904, the first hydropower companies began operating in Niagara Falls, Ontario, and by 1910, they were

Michael Faraday discovered that when a magnet was moved near a wire, it created an electric current. This discovery led to the technology that then led to hydroelectric power plants.

SIR ADAM BECK

In 1905, Adam Beck, the mayor of London, Ontario, urged the Conservative Party to promise free water power from Niagara Falls during the party's election campaign. After winning the election, the Conservative Party immediately went to work on finding a way to keep its promise. Part of the plan included naming Beck chairman of the newly formed Ontario Hydro Electric Power Commission. It was the world's first publicly owned utility. Under Beck's leadership, the Ontario Power Commission took on its first major project, building an 110,000-volt transmission line from Niagara Falls to 14 southwestern Ontario municipalities, including Toronto. The line was completed in October 1910, and Beck held a ceremony to switch on the power in what is now Kitchener, Ontario. By 1914, the Ontario Power Commission supplied power to more than 100 municipalities. It wasn't long before the commission began to experience a power shortage. Beck looked for new ways to generate hydropower. By 1917, work began on the Queenston-Chippawa power project. When it opened in 1921, it was the world's largest power station. The station was later renamed Sir Adam Beck I, in honour of its founder. Today, the plant generates about 2 percent of Ontario's electricity.

transmitting to Ontario Hydro, an electrical power company. There were also hydropower plants in nearly every province. Hydroelectric facilities continued to be developed throughout the 1920s and 1930s, until World War II (1939–1945) caused development to slow. From 1920 to 1950, Canada received more than 90 percent of its power from hydroelectric sources.

After 1950, fossil fuels took over as our primary source of electricity generation. Then, in the 1970s, Canada experienced a shortage of petroleum for gasoline. This shortage sent us scrambling for alternative sources of energy, such as water power.

Ms. Arnold tells me that burning fossil fuels releases carbon dioxide and other gases into the atmosphere. These gases trap the sun's heat similar to how heat is trapped in a greenhouse. This is known as the greenhouse effect, and the gases are known as greenhouse gases. Many scientists believe adding more greenhouse gases to the atmosphere is increasing the greenhouse

Niagara Falls Hydro produces enough power for 24 million lightbulbs.

effect. This, they believe, is contributing to a gradual warming of the earth's average temperature. That's why water power is such an attractive option. Today, hydropower accounts for more than 60 percent of Canada's electricity, making it Canada's main source of electricity. We have about 500 hydropower facilities, and some are more than 100 years old. Fossil fuels are still an important part of Canada's energy production, but it's important to keep considering alternative energy sources.

CHAPTER 3

At the Dam

I bike along River Parkway, a path for cyclists and walkers. To my left, the river tumbles over rocks in swift-running currents. Ms. Arnold said that fast moving water has kinetic energy, and I know just the place to harness it for electricity: the dam.

Jill O'Malley, the dam's manager, invites me to the top of the dam. It sits 104 metres above the river. "Dams are one of the oldest ways to create electricity from moving water," Ms. O'Malley begins. "They have done a lot to provide power and control water across Canada."

Dams hold back river water. At first, many dams were built to control floods and water crops. Today, many dams are used to generate hydroelectric power. Canada has 10 of the world's 40 largest dams in terms of how much water they can hold. In fact, it's estimated Canada has about 10,000 dams, but most are quite small. Lake Manicouagan in Québec is one of the largest man-made lakes in the world. Like many lakes created by dams, Lake Manicouagan is a reservoir for human use. The lake acts as a giant reservoir for the Manicouagan River. Hydroelectric plants along the river provide power to nearby homes. The lake fills a crater that was formed by a meteor impact about 20 million years ago. When the Daniel-Johnson Dam was

'ROUND AND 'ROUND THE WATER CYCLE

Water is the only natural substance on Earth found in liquid, solid, and gas form. Water constantly shifts between these three states whether on, above, or below Earth's surface. The sun heats surface water and evaporates it. The evaporated water condenses into clouds. Precipitation, such as rain or snow, falls on the ground and mixes with our rivers. River water flows to the oceans or lakes, where it evaporates to repeat the cycle.

built on the Manicouagan River, it filled the crater with water, creating Lake Manicouagan.

"Can a dam be built on any river?" I ask.

Ms. O'Malley shakes her head. "First, we need a river with a steady flow that receives regular precipitation in the form of rain or snow. Second, we need water from mountains and surrounding areas to drain into the river and continue feeding it. Third, we need an elevation drop, such as a waterfall. The higher the drop, the greater the energy potential of the river."

I peer over the edge of the dam to the river below. "How does the dam produce electricity?"

Ms. O'Malley smiles. "The dam itself doesn't produce electricity. The dam is a concrete structure that backs up the flow of the river and creates a lake." She points to our left. "Think of the lake as stored energy. When the dam's gates,

SITE C DAM

It took nearly 40 years to get government approval for the Site C Dam, a proposed hydroelectric dam on the Peace River in British Columbia. The massive dam project is now underway and is expected to begin operation in 2020. Site C will be located about 7 kilometres from Fort John, and it will be the third dam on the Peace River, along with the W.A.C. Bennett Dam and the Peace Canyon Dam. When complete, the Site C Dam will provide enough power for more than 450,000 homes for more than 100 years. In addition, the project will create more than 35,000 jobs over the course of its construction. First Nations in the region have expressed concern the project will damage the environment and are working with project planners to help reduce the impact.

Dams like this one in Bassano, Alberta, help make it possible for many people to live and farm in nearby communities.

known as sluice gates, open, water from the lake rushes down the penstock, or pipe, to spin the turbine. The turbine converts the river's kinetic energy to mechanical energy that runs a generator. The generator converts the mechanical energy to electricity, which is then sent over power lines to your home."

I look at the water tumbling over the dam. "What happens to the water?" I ask.

Ms. O'Malley rubs her hands together. "That's the beauty of water power! Unlike biofuels, which are grown and processed, and fossil fuels, which are mined or drilled, water returns to the river on the downstream side of the dam. It's a free and renewable fuel source that never produces greenhouse gases. Hydropower simply borrows the energy in the water before returning it to the river."

I look at the lake on one side of the dam and the river on the other. "You mean this lake wasn't here before the dam?"

I wonder if all of the windsurfers and water-skiers enjoying the lake today know that.

"Right. The area used to be a river with banks and rocks much like you see on the downstream side of the dam. When the dam was built, the lake flooded everything in its path."

Ms. O'Malley explains that building the dam definitely changed the natural environment of the riverbed, both upstream and downstream. It destroyed the homes of many animals living along the riverbanks. She says that dams also change the water chemistry. The oxygen level of the lake is lower than in the free-flowing river. This change affects the plants and animals living in the river. Fish, such as salmon and steelhead trout, used to migrate upstream for centuries

Dams use the energy of moving water to create electric power. They also create large reservoirs people can use for fun activities, such as fishing.

Fishways are passages that allow fish to swim over or around a dam.

to lay their eggs. Now the dam is blocking their path. Fish must climb a special ladder or use a passage over the dam to swim farther upstream.

Dams also impact the environment by blocking sediment that would otherwise be transported by the river. This trapped sediment slowly fills the lake created by the dam. This blocks sunlight and makes the water murkier, changing the environment for the plants and animals.

I never thought about how water power might affect plants and animals. I guess there are pros and cons to water power, too.

CHAPTER 4

The River Wild

Today I'm about to add another piece to the puzzle. Water storage is a big deal for hydroelectric power plants. If the water is stored in the form of a lake on the upstream side of a dam, electricity can be generated at will. But what if the water isn't stored? Can electricity still be generated?

To answer these questions, I hop on a bus headed for the busy river docks. Joseph Trey has offered to meet me there. He is one of the founders of a company that is making electricity from the river's current. I spot Mr. Trey wearing his ball cap and a light jacket. We board a barge with a giant crane and something that looks like a three-bladed ceiling fan lying on its side.

"You picked a great day to stop by, Zach," Mr. Trey says. "We're deploying another turbine in the river today." He points to the odd-looking fan. "We studied this river very carefully. The size of the turbine's blades is determined by the depth and the speed of the river—the deeper the river, the larger the blades."

"Aren't they in the way of ships that travel the river?" I ask. "And what about the fish?"

"Good questions," Mr. Trey says. "We anchor the turbine to the floor of the river away from the shipping channels. Debris floating on the top of the river floats right over our turbines. Fish and other marine life might get a gentle nudge, but the turbines spin too slowly to injure them."

"How many turbines will you put in this river?" I ask. The river is too murky for me to see the bottom.

Mr. Trey grins. "That's a great question! It's actually something we are still trying to figure out. We are currently testing the effects of different numbers of turbines in the water. More turbines do not always mean more electricity. We also need to determine the best spacing for the turbines. Too close and the turbines interfere

Rivers can move extremely fast. If we can capture this energy, we can use it to generate electricity.

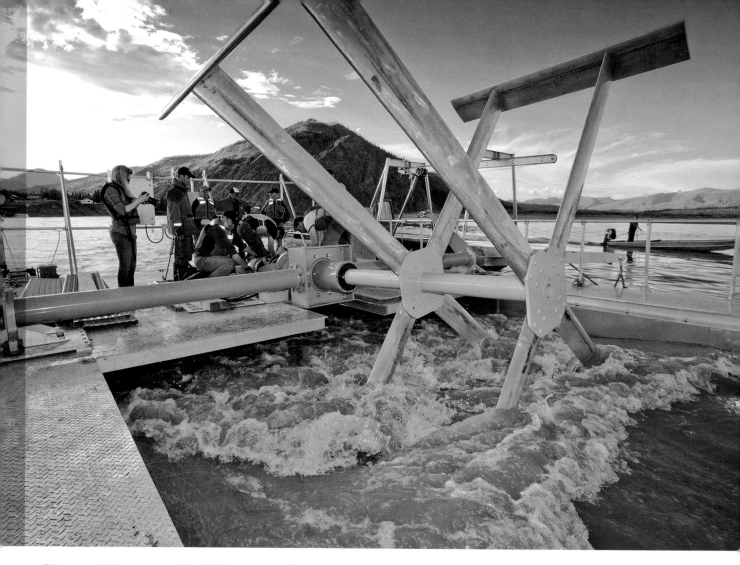

River turbines come in all shapes and sizes. This turbine can generate electricity without using a dam.

with one another. But too far apart, and we waste some of the kinetic energy of the river."

"Mr. Trey, your turbines are really cool. I can see they don't pollute the river and don't create greenhouse gases. But how much electricity do they produce? "

"You and my investors ask the same questions," Mr. Trey says. "An underwater cable connects our turbines to the power grid, where the electricity is distributed to homes and businesses. Each turbine in this river produces about 35 kilowatts of electricity. In contrast, the dam you visited yesterday produces about 200 megawatts—that's more than 5,000 times as much energy. But dams require a

DEMYSTIFYING THE POWER GRID

The power grid transports electricity from its source to your home. A hydroelectric plant turns the energy from waves, tides, or dams into electricity. From the plant, electricity travels to a transmission substation that increases the voltage for long-distance travel. When the high-voltage electricity arrives at another substation approximately 480 kilometres away, its voltage is decreased for use in your home. In Canada, people typically use appliances that require 120 to 240 volts of electricity.

DAM DESTRUCTION

While dams are often built to help provide a power source, some serve other purposes. The 40 Mile Creek dam between Stoney Squaw Mountain and Cascade Mountain was built in 1946 to supply drinking water to the town of Banff, Alberta. However, bacterial contamination has kept it from being used for this purpose since the 1980s. Some people worry the dam could one day collapse due to its age and possible structural defects. Though inspectors have said there is no real threat at the moment, a major natural disaster, such as an earthquake, could cause the dam to fail. If that happened, a large amount of sediment would be released, destroying the creek operations and causing minor flooding to Banff's downtown core. No recent updates have been made to the dam, but inspections are done every three years to ensure the dam's structure is sound. The Town of Banff is working with Parks Canada on plans to take the dam out of use.

substantial change in the environment to build and operate. Our turbines are much less intrusive."

I had no idea so much power could come from rivers. I wonder how we use other bodies of water as energy sources.

The Vermillion Lakes connect to 40 Mile Creek.

CHAPTER 5

The Ebb and Flow of Tides

Today I'm visiting another river that uses tides instead of currents to generate electricity. I'm meeting with Jessica Howard. She studies tides, and I'm hoping she can give me more information about how we use tides to generate power.

Ms. Howard jumps right into the history of tidal power. "More than 1,000 years ago, people ground grain using waterwheels powered by tides instead of river currents. When the tide flowed in, these devices captured tidal water much like dams hold water. The captured water was released to turn the wheel that moved the grinding stones. Fast forward to today. Turbines have replaced waterwheels, but the concept remains the same."

Ms. Howard tells me that structures called tidal barrages capture tidal energy. Tidal barrages are like dams. But instead of harnessing the kinetic energy of a river, they harness the

In the past, humans used tides to power waterwheels. When the tide came in, the moving water rotated the wheel.

kinetic energy of tides. They work best at the mouth of an estuary, where freshwater mixes with seawater. In an estuary, water flows into a narrow channel, which increases its kinetic energy. As the tide rises, the sluice gates of the barrage open. Tidal water flows through the gates and spins the turbines, generating electricity. The sluice gates close, impounding the water, just like a dam. At low tide, the water inside the barrage is higher than outside the barrage. When the sluice gates open, the water rushes out of the barrage back to the ocean, spinning the turbines to generate electricity again.

"Where are tidal barrages found?" I ask.

"Right now, barrages are only in a few countries, including France, Canada, and China," Ms. Howard says. "The world's third-largest tidal power plant is Annapolis Royal. It was built in Nova Scotia's Bay of Fundy in 1984. And Race Rocks, in British

Race Rocks is home to Canada's first tidal current turbine generator.

Columbia, was built in 2006." Ms. Howard tells us it's expensive to build a barrage, and the heavy construction equipment emits greenhouse gases. The barrage also changes water levels and animal life in the tidal area. "The water may become cloudy with silt and other particles. And the barrage blocks boats and ships that transport goods. But there are other tidal options!" Ms. Howard adds.

Another tidal energy option is an offshore lagoon in open water. The offshore lagoon must have a large difference in the height of the water between high and low tide. This works in the same way as the barrage, but it does not affect estuaries at all.

Tidal turbines work very similarly to river turbines. This tidal turbine at Annapolis Royal generates enough power for more than 4,000 homes each year.

"But the tidal stream option is my favourite," Ms. Howard says. "Tidal energy is very predictable. Two high tides occur every day, approximately 12 hours and 25 minutes apart. Yet, not all locations are suitable for tidal systems. The shape of an area's coastline can change tidal flow and the timing of the tides. The mouth of this river happens to be an ideal location, as the river opens into the ocean. Underwater turbines generate electricity using the tides."

Wait. I'm confused. "What's the difference between your tidal stream technology and the river current turbines I visited yesterday?"

Ms. Howard shrugs. "The turbines you saw yesterday use kinetic energy from the river's current, and we use kinetic energy from tides. The size of our turbines and their placement underwater might be different, too, based on the speed and depth of the water. Both kinds of turbines pivot on their posts to catch the flow of the water. But the tidal turbines turn almost 180 degrees to catch the incoming and outgoing tides."

WHAT CAUSES TIDES?

As the moon rotates around Earth, it exerts some gravitational pull on our planet. As it pulls on the nearest oceans, the moon creates a high tide. On the opposite side of Earth, another high tide occurs. The sun's gravity also tugs at Earth. Its force is weaker than the moon's because it is farther away. About twice a month, during full and new moons, the moon is between the sun and Earth. Together the sun and the moon tug extra hard at Earth's oceans, creating higher-than-normal tides.

"Do these turbines hurt the fish?" I ask.

Ms. Howard shakes her head. "Our turbines rotate very slowly, similar to river current turbines. At most, our turbines might bump a fish out of the way. Ships and floating debris pass right over."

So we use the same basic technology to harness energy from river currents and tides. But tidal energy isn't the only energy we can get from the ocean.

CHAPTER 6

Riding the Waves

For my next stop, I'm visiting an experimental wave energy facility in British Columbia. According to my research, the western coasts of Scotland, northern Canada, southern Africa, and the northeastern and northwestern coasts of the United States have great wave energy potential. Scientists calculate the energy in a wave with three measurements: the height of the wave, the length of the wave crest (the top of the wave), and the space between waves. Taller, longer, and faster waves mean more energy.

The surf pounds behind me, and the wind tangles my hair as I introduce myself to Dr. Trevor Roberts. He studies physics, including wave energy. His tanned and lined face reminds me of a veteran surfer.

"Thanks for talking with me today, Dr. Roberts," I say. "I'm hoping you can teach me about wave energy."

"My favourite topic," he says. "Although wave energy is still experimental, it has the potential to make a terrific contribution

Huge waves like this one have a lot of energy. Scientists are working on technology that could harness this energy for human use.

to the world's renewable energy. In fact, it could supply as much as 10 percent of the world's electricity needs."

"So British Columbia has excellent wave potential?" I ask.

"That's right," Dr. Roberts says. "Each year, British Columbia produces about 37,000 megawatts of wave energy, compared to only 4,000 megawatts of tidal current energy."

I once heard one of my science teachers talking about wave technologies. I ask Dr. Roberts to tell me more about them.

"There are five basic technologies to extract energy from waves." He pulls out a chart from his backpack. "One type is point absorbers. These are buoys that float on the water but are attached to the ocean floor. The kinetic energy of the buoys bobbing on the waves becomes electrical energy. Each buoy generates about 500 kilowatts of electricity. Our 200 buoys should be able to generate 100 megawatts of electricity. That's enough to power 24,900 homes."

I look out over the ocean. It's hard to imagine that the waves I'm seeing could produce so much power.

"The second technology is called an overtopping device," Dr. Roberts continues. He points to the second drawing on the chart. "Waves lift water over a barrier and fill a reservoir. The water in the reservoir drains through a turbine that generates electricity."

"The overtopping device sounds like a floating dam," I say.

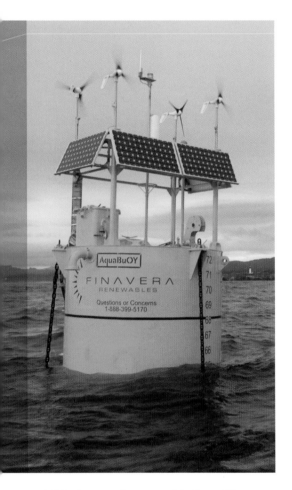

This buoy rises and falls with the ocean's waves. The motion powers a turbine inside the buoy to generate electricity.

"Exactly. You've learned a lot." Dr. Roberts ploughs ahead and points to the third picture. "Attenuators are devices that look a bit like snakes that ride the waves. Each snake has multiple sections that move with the waves. Attenuators convert the kinetic energy of the sections to electricity."

Dr. Roberts pauses. "Still with me?"

I nod, squinting hard at the pictures.

"The first three devices float on top of the water," Dr. Roberts says, pointing to a fourth picture on his chart. "But oscillating water columns are half in and half out of the water. Above the water, air fills the top part of the device. Incoming waves raise the water level below the surface. This extra water squeezes the air through a turbine, which spins to generate electricity. As the strength of the wave passes, the water level in the device decreases. Less water decreases the air pressure. The air is pulled through the turbine for more electricity."

WIND FORECASTING

You've probably heard of weather forecasting, but what about wind forecasting? A program through Hydro-Québec and Environment Canada develops models of wind patterns. Wind makes waves. If scientists can determine when wave-making winds will blow, they will be able to determine the best locations for wave-operated power systems. To understand how winds impact hydroelectricity production, scientists are examining past wind patterns and predictions of future wind patterns to create a huge bank of information for renewable energy experts.

Waves are a source of kinetic energy. This energy can be captured in many different ways.

The last picture on Dr. Roberts' chart looks like an upside-down pendulum. "Let me guess what this one does," I say.

He hands me the chart. "Give it a whirl!"

"The upside-down pendulum moves with the back-and-forth motion of the waves."

Dr. Roberts nods. "We call that surge."

"Okay, the waves surge and force the lever back and forth. The lever is connected to a motor. The motor turns kinetic energy into mechanical energy. Then, a generator turns the mechanical energy into electricity."

Dr. Roberts smiles. "How would you like to work for us in a few years?"

CHAPTER 7

Shallow/Warm, Deep/Cold

Today I'm travelling outside of Canada to visit a renewable energy centre in Hawaii. I want to ask the centre's manager, Scott Meyers, some questions about a brand-new type of ocean energy.

"Welcome to our pilot plant," Mr. Meyers says. The plant is right next to the beach, and he is wearing a colourful Hawaiian shirt and flip-flops. "We're one of the world's leading test facilities for an exciting new type of hydropower called OTEC."

"Does OTEC stand for something special?" I ask.

"**O**cean **T**hermal **E**nergy **C**onversion." Mr. Meyers grins at my blank look. "Tides and waves are not the only sources of energy in the ocean. OTEC uses the temperature difference between warm water at the ocean's surface and cold water 1,000 metres below. Our experimental plant has the ability to produce steady energy without waiting for tides to ebb and flow."

We can harness energy from more than just the ocean's waves.

I look out to sea. I remember 96.5 percent of the earth's water is in its oceans. "Why isn't OTEC used all over the world?"

"Excellent question," Mr. Meyers says. "For OTEC to work, the surface water needs to be at least 20 degrees Celsius warmer than the deep water. While our oceans are full of areas that could work for OTEC, most of them are too far from shore. The distance makes the conversion to electricity expensive and difficult. Coastal areas with a tropical climate have the best chance of success. Seasons make a difference, too. Surface water is colder in the winter, so potential OTEC areas are even fewer."

"I get it now, Mr. Meyers, but how do you make electricity from the cold and warm ocean water?"

Mr. Meyers kicks four piles of sand together to illustrate his explanation. He points to the first pile of sand. "Here we have a container for warm surface seawater. First, we pump the seawater in. Then we send it to a second container called a flash evaporator that reduces the pressure." He gestures to the second pile of sand.

"As the pressure drops, the water vapourizes to steam. The volume of the steam is now greater than the seawater. It needs to move out of its small container." He points to the third pile of sand. "The steam blasts past the turbine that spins to generate electricity, and into a fourth container. Here, cold seawater pumped from more than 1,000 metres below surrounds the last container and condenses the steam back to salt-free water."

"Salt-free water?" I pause to think about what Mr. Meyers is telling me. "So you're saying that ocean thermal energy conversion not only generates electricity, but it also creates drinking water?"

Mr. Meyers claps me on the back. "That's exactly what OTEC does!"

HYDROTHERMAL VENTS

The earth's crust is made up of giant plates. Since oceans cover much of Earth's surface, many of these plates meet underwater. As the plates shift, small cracks form. Seawater trickles through the cracks to the earth's core of hot magma. The seawater becomes super-heated to 370 degrees Celsius and returns through hydrothermal vents 2,300 metres deep. The extreme pressure at these depths prevents the water from boiling. If we can channel the energy of hydrothermal vents to the surface, they might become the next source of renewable water power.

Wow! I knew water was important to humans' survival, but I had no idea we could use water power for so much. Like all energy sources, water power has its pros and cons. But it is clean and renewable. It is already an important source of energy for people across Canada and around the world. I'm excited to see what the future holds for water power.

One day we may be able to use hot water spewed out by hydrothermal vents deep in the ocean to generate electricity.

CHAPTER 8

Your Turn

You've had a chance to follow Zach as he conducted his research. Now it's time to think about what you've learned. You have studied the pros and cons of dams and tidal barrages. These structures can produce a lot of power, but they can also change the environment in which they are built. Free-flowing systems, such as river currents and tidal turbines, don't have as many negative effects on the environment, but they don't produce nearly enough power on their own to meet our energy needs. You have also learned about experimental ocean energy technologies, such as waves and ocean thermal energy conversions. While these don't play a large role in our water power use right now, they may be an important part of our energy future. Scientists and engineers keep exploring new and better ways to make use of water power. Maybe you'll make the next big discovery!

YOU DECIDE

1. Do you think the positive aspects of water power outweigh the negative aspects? Why or why not?

2. Which water power technology discussed in Zach's journal do you think is most promising? Why?

3. What can you do to cut down on your energy use? Think about technology and behavioural changes.

4. If you had enough money to invest in one type of water power research, which project would you choose? Why?

5. How big of a role do you think water power will play in our future energy production?

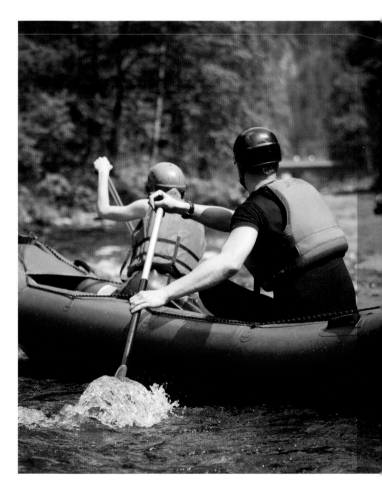

Water is needed for life on Earth. It has played an important role in our energy production for thousands of years. Soon, it may have an even greater role.

GLOSSARY

attenuators: Ocean energy devices that capture wave energy to convert it to electricity.

barrage: A low dam built across an estuary to capture the energy produced by tides.

estuary: A body of water formed by freshwater rivers and streams emptying into the salt water of the ocean.

fossil fuels: Energy sources that developed from the remains of animals and plants.

generator: A machine that converts mechanical energy into electricity.

gravity: The force that attracts a body toward the centre of the earth.

hydroelectric: Generating electricity from flowing water that drives a turbine.

kilowatts: One thousand watts of electrical power.

kinetic energy: The energy a substance in motion contains.

megawatts: One million watts of electrical power, or 1,000 kilowatts.

non-renewable: Something that cannot be replaced by natural environmental cycles as quickly as we are using it.

oscillating: Moving or swinging back and forth in a regular rhythm.

penstock: Large tubes that lead water from a reservoir above a dam to the turbines that spin to generate electricity.

renewable: Something that can be replaced by cycles in nature or the environment.

reservoir: A place where something is collected, especially a liquid.

sluice gates: A sliding gate that controls the flow of water.

turbine: A machine that spins to power a machine that generates electricity.

voltage: The measurement of the energy contained within an electric circuit at a given point.

Make a Turbine

You will need an empty, cardboard, 2-litre milk carton. Use a nail to punch one hole in the exact middle of the top of the carton. Put a piece of string through the hole so you can hang the carton. Punch two additional holes in the bottom right corner and the bottom left corner. Put heavy tape over these two holes. Hang the carton from a tree outside. Fill the carton with water. Rip the tape off one corner. What happens? Rip the tape off the other corner. What happens? Explain what is happening with the concepts you learned in this book.

Where Does the Water Cycle Begin?

Show your friends, teachers, parents, and coaches the picture of the water cycle in Chapter Three of this book. Ask each person the following questions:

- Where does the water cycle begin?

- What is the best source of hydropower?

- Make one chart for each question summarizing the responses. Graph your results.

Do You Conserve or Waste Energy at Home?

Draw a map of your home. Visit each room to find the items that use energy, such as lights, the thermostat to regulate heat or air conditioning, televisions, computers, and appliances. Indicate whether these items were on or off when you visited each room. Ask your parents if your home uses renewable forms of energy, such as hydropower. Can you think of ways to conserve energy in your home?

What can you do in your home to help conserve energy?

SELECTED BIBLIOGRAPHY

"Dams & Diversions." *Environment Canada*. Canada.gc.ca, n.d. Web. Accessed April 3, 2014.

"Hydropower Timeline." *Centre for Energy*. Canadian Centre for Energy Information, 2014. Web. Accessed April 4, 2014.

"Niagara Falls Hydro." *Visiting Niagara Falls*. Visiting-niagara-falls.com, 2012. Web. Accessed April 5, 2014.

"Site C Clean Energy Project." *BC Hydro*. BC Hydro, 2014. Web. Accessed April 6, 2014.

"Tidal Current Energy Demonstration Project: Renewable Energy for Race Rocks." *Race Rocks Ecological Reserve*. Lester B. Pearson College, n.d. Web. Accessed April 3, 2014.

FURTHER INFORMATION

Books

Gardner, Robert. *Energy: Green Science Projects about Solar, Wind, and Water Power*. Berkeley Heights, NJ: Enslow, 2011.

Goodman, Polly. *Understanding Water Power*. Pleasantville, NY: Gareth Stevens, 2011.

Spilsbury, Richard. *Water, Wave, and Tidal Power*. New York: PowerKids Press, 2012.

Winnick, Nick. *Green Power*. Minneapolis, MN: AV^2 by Weigl, 2011.

Websites

https://canadahydro.ca
The Canadian Hydro Power Association site has facts about using water as an energy source.

http://energyquest.ca.gov/index.html
The Energy Quest website contains lots of great information on energy, including a story, movies, and more.

http://www.centreforenergy.com/AboutEnergy/Hydro
The Centre for Energy has charts, illustrations, videos, and information about hydro power, its history, and its impact on the environment.

INDEX